Energy from Fossil Fuels

Robert Snedden

Heinemann Library
Chicago, Illinois

© 2002 Reed Educational & Professional Publishing
Published by Heinemann Library,
an imprint of Reed Educational & Professional Publishing,
Chicago, Illinois

Customer Service 888-454-2279

Visit our website at www.heinemannlibrary.com

Text and cover designed by Celia Floyd
Illustrated by Jeff Edwards and Alan Fraser

Originated by Ambassador Litho Ltd.
Printed in Hong Kong by Wing King Tong

06 05 04 03 02
10 9 8 7 6 5 4 3

Library of Congress Cataloging-in-Publication Data
Snedden, Robert.
    Energy from fossil fuels / by Robert Snedden.
       p. cm. -- (Essential energy)
    Includes bibliographical references and index.
    ISBN 1-57572-442-1 (lib. bdg.)
    1. Fossil fuels--Juvenile literature. [1. Fossil fuels. 2. Power
resources.]   I. Title.
  TP318.3 .S54 2001
  553.2--dc21
                                        2001000101

Acknowledgments
The author and publishers are grateful to the following for permission to reproduce copyright material:
Corbis, pp.4, 9, 18, 19; Hulton Deutsch, p.5; Science Photo Library, pp.6, 7, 11, 15, 21, 23, 25, 26, 27, 29, 30, 36, 40, 41; Robert Harding Picture Library, pp.8, 33; South American Pictures, p.13; Mary Evans Picture Library, pp.14, 20, 22; Hulton Getty, pp.16, 17; Camera Press, pp.28, 42; Austin J. Brown/Aviation Picture Library, p.35; Environmental Images, pp.37, 38, 39; Paul Popper Ltd., p.43.

Cover photograph reproduced with permission of Photodisc.

Some words are shown in bold, **like this.** You can find out what they mean by looking in the glossary.

Contents

Ancient Sunlight

Energy makes things happen. It is the driving force of the universe. Without energy, there would be no universe at all. Scientists define *energy* as "the ability to do work." For a scientist, any activity involves work because all activities involve energy. Even when you are asleep, your body is still at work, breaking down the food you eat, carrying out repairs, and making new **cells.** A rock sitting motionless on the ground contains **chemical energy** that holds together the **atoms** it is made of and the atomic energy that holds together the particles that make up those atoms.

Life and energy

All life needs a source of energy. Most of the energy used by life on Earth comes from the Sun. In the remarkable process of **photosynthesis,** green plants and some **microorganisms** capture the Sun's energy and use it to make food. The food that plants make for themselves becomes, in turn, the source of energy for all of Earth's other organisms. These organisms eat either plants or animals that have eaten plants.

Without the Sun, Earth would be a dark and lifeless rock.

People and energy

Over time, people have developed new ways to find and control sources of energy. In ancient times, people had only the strength of their own muscles to rely on. Later, the invention of agriculture and the domestication of animals provided another source of energy, because animals could be used to plow fields and transport goods. Learning how to use fire made it possible for people to make pottery, forge metals, and cook food. Using the energy of the wind to power sailing ships allowed people to travel along rivers and across oceans.

A train powered by steam uses energy from the Sun that has been stored in coal.

With the discovery of **fossil fuels,** people found a new way to use the energy of the Sun. Coal, **petroleum,** and **natural gas** all contain energy from the Sun. This energy was trapped by living plants and microorganisms many millions of years ago. Fossil fuels, and coal in particular, powered the **Industrial Revolution.** This period of rapid economic change eventually led to the high-technology society we live in today.

We still rely a great deal on the ancient energy trapped in fossil fuels. We use the energy of petroleum in our aircraft and road vehicles. Many of us use natural gas to cook our food. Coal, oil, and gas are all used to provide the energy we need to generate electricity in power stations. This book tells the story of fossil fuels—how they are formed, how we find them, the many ways we use them, and how they affect the world around us.

Energy Supply

We use different forms of energy to provide light and heat, to operate machinery, to prepare our food, to take us from place to place, and to make things we need. All the available energy we have makes up our energy supply.

Sometimes we get energy directly. For example, when we pluck an apple from a tree and eat it, we are making use of energy from the Sun that the tree has trapped and stored in the apple. This energy supplies a part of the energy that our bodies need. Often we use energy indirectly, such as when we burn coal in a power station to heat water and turn it into steam. The steam is then used to spin a **turbine** that generates electricity, which we can put to many uses.

The Trans-Alaskan oil pipeline runs over 700 miles (1,200 kilometers) across Alaska.

Essential fossil fuels

The world's chief sources of energy are, in order of importance, **fossil fuels,** water power, and nuclear energy. Solar, wind, tidal, and **geothermal energy** also provide some of our energy needs. More than 85 percent of the energy produced by businesses and governments comes from the fossil fuels **petroleum,** coal, and **natural gas.** These sources are called fossil fuels because they formed over millions of years from the fossilized remains of prehistoric plants.

The supply of fossil fuels is limited. Fossil fuels are a **nonrenewable resource.** This means that once they are used, they cannot be recycled or replaced, and eventually they will run out. Scientists and engineers are working to find ways of getting the most from our fossil fuel resources and to develop other sources of energy.

Petroleum: Petroleum alone supplies 40 percent of the world's energy, mostly to provide energy for transportation and heating. Most petroleum comes from deep underground as a liquid called **crude oil.** Refineries process the crude oil, breaking it down into kerosene, gasoline, and other useful products.

Coal: More than a quarter (26 percent) of the world's energy production comes from coal. Coal is used to manufacture steel, to produce the energy for steam engines, and to generate electricity. In many parts of the world, coal is used to heat people's homes.

Natural gas: Natural gas supplies about 21 percent of the world's energy needs. It is used to generate electricity, for heating and cooking, and sometimes for lighting.

Problems to solve

While fossil fuels have helped shape our high-technology society, they continue to cause many problems. Spills from oil tankers pollute coastlines. Illnesses from breathing coal dust and accidents make coal mining a dangerous occupation. When fossil fuels are burned, they give off carbon dioxide, a **greenhouse gas**, which many people believe is causing Earth to get warmer. Burning coal releases sulfur **compounds** and other impurities that cause **acid rain** and pollute the air. These problems cannot be ignored, and scientists are working hard to search for answers.

Coal provides the energy for the fierce heat needed to make steel in a blast furnace.

Photosynthesis

The process of making **fossil fuels** begins with sunlight. When plants use **photosynthesis** to change the Sun's energy into food, they provide the fuels that power our cars, heat our homes, and cook our food. Photosynthesis is a very important process.

In photosynthesis, green plants, algae, and some bacteria capture the energy of sunlight and use it to form glucose, a simple sugar, out of carbon dioxide and water. Photosynthesis, then, indirectly supplies almost all of the energy used by living things on Earth.

Chloroplasts

The entire process of photosynthesis takes place in chloroplasts, tiny green structures found mainly inside the leaf **cells** of green plants. Chloroplasts are extremely tiny and are disk-shaped. Each chloroplast contains chlorophyll, the pigment that gives the plant its green color, and other chemicals necessary for photosynthesis. During photosynthesis, chlorophyll captures the energy of sunlight and uses it to split water **molecules.**

Microscopic structures inside a plant cell allow it to capture energy from sunlight.

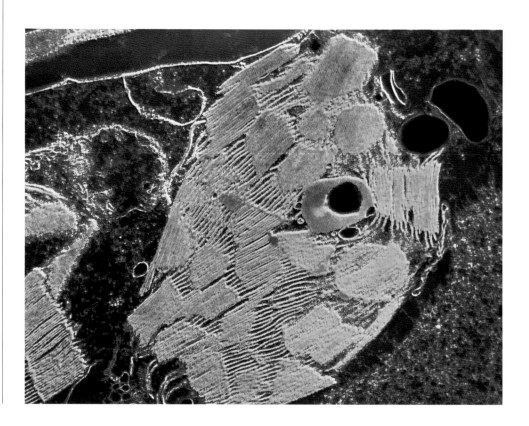

The chemical reactions involved in photosynthesis occur in two stages. During the first stage, sunlight is used to split water into oxygen, hydrogen **ions,** and electrons. During the second stage, which does not require sunlight, the hydrogen ions and electrons are used to change carbon dioxide into **carbohydrates.** The process can be summarized in the following chemical formula:

$$6CO_2 + 12H_2O + sunlight \rightarrow C_6H_{12}O_6 + 6H_2O + 6O_2$$
(carbon dioxide + water + sunlight $\rightarrow$ glucose + water + oxygen)

Most of the glucose that forms during photosynthesis is stored as starch in the chloroplasts. As animals eat the plant's leaves, they meet their basic energy needs by consuming the energy that has been stored by the plant. Photosynthesis, changing the Sun's energy into food, is essential for life because it is the only way new energy can be introduced on Earth. Without sunlight, life on Earth would be limited to communities of simple organisms.

An incidental benefit

Oxygen, a product of photosynthesis, is very important to nearly all living organisms. Oxygen is needed for us to get energy from the food that we eat. Most of the oxygen in the atmosphere comes from photosynthesis.

Together, Earth's plants use sunlight to produce billions of tons of sugar every second.

From Forests to Fossil Fuel

Around 365 million years ago, during a time in Earth's history called the Carboniferous Period, the first forests appeared. These swampy forests were unlike anything we know today because they had no trees. Instead, there were tree-sized club mosses and ferns, some with trunks over 98 feet (30 meters) tall, all competing for light. Much of what is now North America and Europe was covered in fern forests. These forests were probably gloomy places, home to giant cockroaches, dragonflies as big as seagulls, scorpions, spiders, and amphibians in the muddy forest pools. There were no flowering plants or birds to provide color and song.

Peat

During the Carboniferous Period, there was not enough oxygen in the muddy forest pools to support the tiny **decomposers** that usually break down dead plants and animals. As a result, when the swamp-forest plants died, they did not completely decay, but were instead buried under layer upon layer of mud. Over the years, the partly decomposed plant matter was compressed into a substance called **peat.** Peat still forms today where the conditions are right. In many places, it is cut and dried for fuel.

Coal is formed over millions of years as ancient plant remains are compressed deep underground.

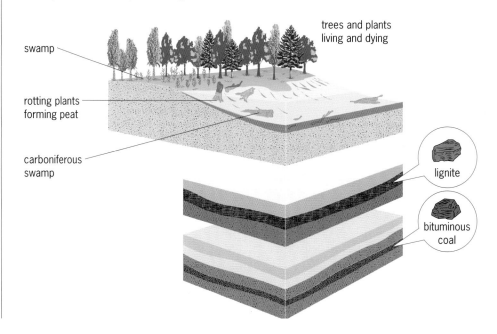

swamp

trees and plants living and dying

rotting plants forming peat

carboniferous swamp

lignite

bituminous coal

Sedimentary rocks

Over time, the peat deposits were buried under sand or other rocky materials. As these **mineral** deposits built up, the increasing pressure turned the deeper layers into such rocks as sandstone and shale. Rocks formed from mineral deposits in this way are called **sedimentary rocks.** As the temperature and pressure grew, the weight of the rock layers pressing down on the peat began the process that transformed it into coal.

Coal formation

Buried peat deposits first produce a dark brown type of coal called lignite. Plant material is still recognizable in lignite. As pressure begins to build, the lignite turns into harder bituminous coal. Intense pressure at the deepest levels changes bituminous coal into anthracite, the hardest of coals. As you would expect, anthracites are the oldest coals, found deepest in the ground, and lignites are the youngest. Anthracites are more than 300 million years old, whereas some lignites formed from plants growing within the last million years or so.

Coal composition

Coal is often called a mineral. However, minerals have a fixed chemical formula—a special combination of ingredients. Coal is chiefly composed of carbon, hydrogen, nitrogen, oxygen, and sulfur, but the actual amounts of each element can vary greatly. Coal is usually classified according to how much carbon it contains. Anthracites are about 98 percent carbon, while lignites have a carbon content as low as 30 percent. Anthracites and bituminous coal have a moisture content of about 1 percent. Lignites are made up of as much as 45 percent moisture. The way coal is used depends on its chemical formula and on how much moisture it contains.

These are samples of anthracite, the oldest, hardest coal.

Compact coal

Over six feet (two meters) of compacted plant matter will eventually produce a **seam** of bituminous coal about three inches (eight centimeters) thick.

Sea-Life Energy

Scientists believe that **petroleum,** or **crude oil,** was formed from the remains of tiny organisms that lived in the world's oceans millions of years ago. They came to this conclusion because they found carbon **compounds** in oil that could have come only from once-living organisms.

Oil formation

Millions of tiny organisms live in shallow water near the coasts or close to the surface in the deep ocean. As these organisms die, their remains sink through the water to settle among the sand and silt on the seafloor. Gradually, over a long period of time, this mixture of sediments and **organic** material thickens.

As the deposits become thicker, increasingly high temperatures and pressure squeeze the lower layers together to form **sedimentary rock.** These extreme conditions cause chemical changes in the organic remains, forming a waxy substance called kerogen. At a temperature of around 212° F (100° C), kerogen separates into liquid oil and **natural gas.** At greater depths, where the temperature rises above 392° F (200° C), the chemical bonds holding the **molecules** of the oil together begin to break down. So, if the temperature is lower than 212° F (100° C), little oil forms. If it is higher than 392° F (200° C), the oil breaks down. This temperature range is called the oil window.

Oil can be reached only by drilling through the impervious rock layers, under which it is trapped.

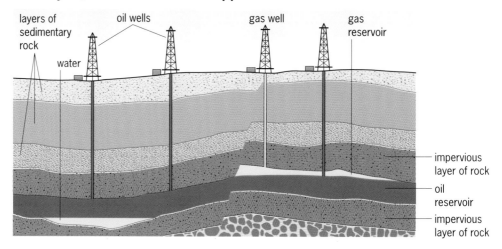

layers of sedimentary rock

oil wells

gas well

gas reservoir

water

impervious layer of rock

oil reservoir

impervious layer of rock

Pores and reservoirs

Sedimentary rock is filled with tiny cracks and holes, called pores. Oil and gas travel up through these pores. This probably happens because water in the rock pushes the oil upward or because pressure from the rocks above squeezes the oil into the pores. As the oil and gas move up through the pores, they eventually reach a layer of **impervious** rock that they cannot pass through. They collect beneath it in a layer of **porous** rock called a reservoir.

Some reservoirs form near Earth's surface, but most are hidden deep underground. Although all oil reserves began beneath the seafloor, movements of Earth's crust over millions of years have meant that many places that were once seafloor are now dry land. For example, more than 100 million years ago, the deserts of the Middle East were beneath the Tethys Sea. The movements of Earth's crust can sometimes bring oil reservoirs to the surface, and the oil appears on the ground as **seepages** or springs. In Venezuela and Trinidad, lakes of oil have collected at the surface.

These oil rigs are located on Lake Maracaibo in Venezuela.

A continuing process

Oil formation continues today as sediment beneath the seafloor undergoes the same conditions of heat and pressure that formed oil millions of years ago. However, it will take millions more years to complete the process, and we are using oil much faster than it is being formed.

King Coal

Coal is a useful fuel. The amount of **heat energy** produced when a certain amount of coal is burned is called its **heating value.** High-moisture coals, such as lignites, have a lower heating value than anthracites and bituminous coals. Bituminous coals are by far the most plentiful and widely used types of coal. They have a slightly higher heating value than anthracites and are the only coals suitable for making **coke.** Anthracites burn too slowly for industrial purposes such as generating electricity, so bituminous coals are preferred.

Coal has many impurities, such as sulfur. As coal is burned, most of the sulfur combines with oxygen to form sulfur dioxide gas. High-sulfur coals can cause serious pollution problems if they are burned without removing the sulfur dioxide. Some of the ash left behind when coal is burned may also escape into the air. Filters are used to trap the ash in smokestacks to prevent it from reaching the air.

Native Americans in what is now British Columbia burned coal for warmth.

Using coal

In many parts of North America, Europe, and Asia coal is still used to heat homes and other buildings. Anthracites are the cleanest-burning coals, and for this reason, they are the best coals for heating homes. Unfortunately, anthracites are also the most expensive coals. So bituminous coals are often used instead to heat factories and other large commercial buildings.

Raw materials

The energy from coal is used to make a variety of products, and many substances made from coal are used as raw materials. Coke, for example, is made by heating bituminous coal to about 1,832° F (1,100° C) in an airtight oven. Keeping oxygen out prevents the coal from burning. The heat causes some of the impurities in the coal to boil off as gases. Coke is used mainly in the manufacture of iron and steel.

When some of the gases produced during coking cool, they turn into liquid ammonia and coal tar. Further processing produces a light oil from some of the other gases. Ammonia, coal tar, and light oil are used to make such products as drugs, dyes, and fertilizers. Coal tar is also used for roofing and road surfacing.

Coking also produces coal gas. This burns like **natural gas** but it has a lower heating value. It also gives off large amounts of soot as it burns. Coal gas is sometimes recycled to provide heat for coking. It is possible to make high-energy gas and liquid fuels, such as gasoline and fuel oil, from coal, but this is a costly and complex process.

First fires

We will never know who first discovered that coal could be burned to provide heat. The world's first coal industry was established in China by the 300s C.E. The coking process was developed by brewers in during the 1600s. In 1709, Abraham Darby, an English ironmaker, devised a way to produce coke commercially and began to use it to **smelt** iron.

This coking plant is located in Pennsylvania.

Discovering Petroleum

The word *petroleum* comes from two Latin words meaning "rock" and "oil." People have been using oil from rocks for thousands of years. The ancient Egyptians coated mummies with pitch, a sticky black substance made from coal tar. Pitch was also used in ancient times to make wooden ships watertight. Centuries before European settlers arrived, Native Americans used **crude oil** for fuel and to make medicine. Remains of oil wells in the eastern United States prove that Native Americans knew how to get oil from underground deposits.

By the mid-1700s, North American colonists had found many oil **seepages** in New York, Pennsylvania, and West Virginia. Some wells that were dug for salt produced oil, which at the time was regarded as a nuisance. During the 1840s, Abraham Gesner, a Canadian **geologist,** discovered kerosene. With the growing popularity of this fuel, which could be made from coal or oil, oil became more valuable.

Edwin Drake's oil well was in Titusville, Pennsylvania.

Birth of the oil industry
In 1859, Edwin L. Drake, a former railway conductor, drilled a well near Titusville, Pennsylvania. People called the well Drake's Folly, not believing that he would find anything. However, Drake struck oil. Wooden **derricks** sprang up all over the hills of Pennsylvania as other prospectors began to drill wells nearby. Within three years, so much oil was being produced that the price of a barrel fell from $20 to 10 cents. At first, wagons and river barges carried the oil to refineries, but soon railway lines were laid to transport the growing amounts of oil. In 1865, the first successful oil pipeline was built to carry oil five miles (eight kilometers) from Titusville to the nearest railway link. Within 10 years, a 62-mile (100-kilometer) pipe was delivering oil to Pittsburgh, Pennsylvania.

The industry grows

In 1860, Italy became the next country to produce oil. Canada, Poland, Russia, Venezuela, Indonesia, Mexico, and several other countries soon followed. The first oil fields of the Middle East were discovered in Iran in 1908, in Iraq in 1927, and in Saudi Arabia in 1938.

At first, kerosene was the chief product of the petroleum industry. Gasoline was seen as a useless by-product and was often dumped straight into rivers. During the early 1900s, this changed with the arrival of electric lights and the automobile. Suddenly, gasoline was not useless any more. The introduction of the thermal-cracking process in 1913 meant that the larger hydrocarbon **molecules** in petroleum could be split into smaller gasoline molecules. This meant that more gasoline could be made from crude oil.

During World War II, armed forces relied heavily on supplies of petroleum.

World War I (1914–1918) caused a huge increase in demand for petroleum fuels to power ships, trains, trucks, and aircraft. After the war, many more farmers in the United States and Europe began to use tractors and other equipment powered by oil.

World War II (1939–1945) caused another huge increase in the production of petroleum, because more oil products were needed for fuels and lubricants. The demand for petroleum products kept on growing, even after the war.

Natural Gas

Natural gas is easily distributed in pipelines and can be used for a wide variety of purposes, such as heating and cooking. Natural gas has several advantages over other fuels. It can be lit or put out quickly, and it can be burned in large or small amounts. This allows people to make small temperature adjustments. Compared with coal and oil, natural gas produces much less pollution when it is burned.

Finding natural gas

Natural gas forms beneath Earth's surface over millions of years as part of the same process that forms **petroleum**. This means that oil and natural gas are often found together. The natural gas lies on top of the oil deposit or is dissolved in it.

Natural gas is found in **porous** rocks such as limestone and sandstone. A dome of **nonporous** rock, such as that which forms over a **salt dome,** forms a cap over the gas-bearing rock, trapping the gas. The gas cannot escape until a drill opens a hole through the solid rock.

Drilling for gas is done the same way as drilling for oil. The most common method is **rotary** drilling. **Offshore** gas wells are drilled in water as much as 7,800 feet (2,400 meters) deep. Offshore drillers work from a barge, a movable rig, or a fixed platform. Offshore drilling costs more than drilling on land, but it is usually much more productive. Some of the richest offshore gas-producing areas are in the waters off of the Gulf Coast of the United States and in the North Sea, around Europe.

A crew drilling for natural gas fits drill pipes together.

The gas industry

The natural gas industry began in the United States. It grew quickly during the late 1920s with the development of pipes that could carry gas great distances cheaply. Up until the 1960s, little natural gas was available in Europe. But, with the discovery of gas fields in the North Sea and in the former Soviet Union, the natural gas industry expanded rapidly. The world's largest known gas field was found in the Soviet Union in 1966.

Explosive power

In 1967, a hydrogen bomb with an explosive power equivalent to over 26,000 tons of TNT was detonated 4,265 feet (1,300 meters) underground in the San Juan Basin of northwestern New Mexico. The explosion revealed gas deposits that had been trapped in rock formations too hard for normal drilling.

This drilling rig is in the Gulf of Mexico.

Gas distribution

Natural gas has to be cleaned and treated when it leaves the well. It is first taken to an extraction unit where impurities are removed. Next, natural gas may be taken to processing plants, where butane, propane, and ethane can be taken out. The processed natural gas is then pushed through underground transmission pipelines to the people who want to use it.

Gas mains are large pipes connected to the transmission pipelines. Smaller pipes, called service lines, branch off from the gas mains, carrying the gas to people in homes, factories, schools, and other buildings. Pure natural gas has no smell, so a chemical is added to make it smell. This makes gas leaks easier to notice.

Working in a Coal Mine

Thousands of miners, including men, women and children, have been killed in mine accidents. Many thousands have died of lung diseases as a result of breathing in coal dust. All large-scale early mining was done by hand, with miners using picks and bars to remove coal from solid rock. During the 1800s, when demand for coal was soaring, many miners worked underground for more than ten hours a day, six days a week. Once the coal was removed, it was brought to the surface by people or by animals such as dogs and horses.

During the 1800s, children as young as ten wheeled coal from the mines.

During the late 1700s, miners started using explosives to blast coal out of rock. During the late 1700s and 1800s, steam power was used to transport coal and pump water from mines. This greatly improved underground coal mining. Today, most of the work in coal mines is done with machines. Although safety has been improved, coal mining is still a dangerous job.

Modern methods

Today, there are three main ways to reach an underground coal **seam.** If a seam is exposed to the surface, such as on the side of a hill or mountain, a mine can be dug directly into the coal seam. This is the easiest and least expensive method. Otherwise, a slanted opening or a vertical mine shaft has to be dug through the rock to reach the coal seam. Once the miners reach the seam, they use a variety of ways to get the coal out.

In conventional mining, the coal is first cut with a large chainsaw on wheels called an undercutter. Explosives are put into holes drilled into the coal. These blast the coal from the seam. The coal is loaded into a shuttle car that takes it to a conveyor belt for transportation to the surface. The roof of the mine is supported by wooden timbers, steel beams set on posts, or by steel rods anchored into holes drilled in the roof.

In the continuous mining system, a single machine does the job of the undercutter, drills, explosives, and loading machine. Other machines include the boring machine, which cuts or breaks the coal using arms that rotate against the surface of the coal. A ripper, which is similar to an undercutter, cuts the coal using chains and can load the coal that it cuts. A milling or drum miner cuts the coal with drill bits mounted on rotating drums.

Strip mining

Strip mining, or surface mining, began in about 1910 when steam shovels were first being used. Today, 60 percent of all coal is mined by this method. Often the coal deposit is covered by soil, which must first be stripped off. The coal is then broken up by explosives.

In longwall mining, large exposed blocks of coal, 325 to 650 feet (100 to 200 meters) wide, are removed. **Hydraulic jacks** provide roof support during mining. These jacks move forward as the coal is mined and the roof behind the jacks is allowed to collapse. A conveyor belt carries the broken coal to the surface.

No matter how advanced the mining equipment is, mining is a dangerous job.

Searching for Oil

An engraving from the 1800s shows men running from the gusher as Drake's Folly strikes oil.

Before about 1900, oil prospectors drilled where they found an oil **seepage,** and hoped for the best. Their equipment was little more than a pick, a shovel, and perhaps a divining rod—a forked stick that some believed would mysteriously lead them to the right place. During the 1900s, however, oil exploration became more of a scientific process as **geologists** learned how and why oil deposits are formed.

Oil and geology

Oil geologists find oil by studying rock formations. First they select an area that seems promising, such as one with **sedimentary rocks.** Then they create a detailed map using photographs from satellites and aircraft and make observations on the ground. They study the map for signs of possible oil traps. A low bulge might be caused by a **salt dome,** one common type of **petroleum** trap.

Next, the geologists take cores, or cylindrical samples cut through the layers of rock. They study the structure and chemical makeup of the core. **Geophysicists** use special instruments such as gravimeters, magnetometers, and seismographs to locate geological structures that may contain oil.

The gravimeter, or **gravity** meter, measures the pull of gravity at a particular location. Different kinds of rocks have different effects on gravity. For example, **nonporous** rocks tend to increase gravitational pull, while **porous** rocks tend to decrease it. Low readings on a gravimeter signals that there might be rocks containing oil in that location.

A magnetometer measures changes in Earth's **magnetic field.** The magnetic field, like gravity, is affected by the type of rocks beneath the surface. Sedimentary rocks usually have weaker magnetic fields than other types of rock do. This difference helps to identify oil-bearing sedimentary rocks.

Seismographic surveys

A seismograph measures the speed of vibrations that are traveling through Earth, either from an earthquake or from an underground explosion. Geophysicists can map the depth and shape of potential oil traps by recording the changing speed of the vibrations as they travel through rocks. To avoid using explosives, geophysicists will sometimes use a thumper truck that strikes the ground repeatedly with a large metal plate.

Geologists also use seismographic surveys to find oil at sea. A pulse of compressed air or an electronic pulse is sent out from a ship into the water. The waves from this pulse are reflected back from underwater features and are recorded.

Seismographs allow geologists to look for fluids in rock formations under the ground by using a technique called bright spot technology. Highly sensitive recorders pick up changes in the height of the vibration waves as they are reflected from rocks that contain fluids. These variations appear as bright spots on the seismograph.

Thumper trucks are used to search for oil in the desert of Libya.

Drilling for Oil

No matter how thoroughly **geologists** survey an area, there is still only one chance in ten that oil will be found when the drilling begins. There is only 1 chance in 50 that there will be enough oil to balance the cost of removing it.

Preparing the site

A drilling site on land is first leveled and cleared with bulldozers. Roads are built to carry personnel and heavy equipment to the site. Supplies of water and power are provided, along with living quarters for the workers if there are no towns nearby. The oil rig, which is mainly made up of drilling equipment and a **derrick,** will arrive by truck, barge, or aircraft.

Rigging up

Connecting the parts of the oil rig is called rigging up. First, the crew builds the derrick over the place where the well is to be drilled. Derricks range in height from 75 to 195 feet (24 to 60 meters), depending on how deep the oil is believed to be. Hoisting machinery, for raising and lowering the drill in and out of the well hole, is attached to the derrick. Next, the engines that power the drill and other machinery are installed on the rig, as well as different pipes, tanks, pumps, and other equipment. When the drill is attached to hoisting machinery, the hole is dug.

Drilling

There are two main types of drilling: cable-tool and **rotary.** In cable-tool drilling, a steel cable repeatedly raises and drops a heavy cutting tool called a bit. Each time the bit drops, it cuts deeper into the ground. This method is best suited to digging shallow wells in hard rock. Bits may be over 6 feet (2 meters) long and more than 11 inches (30 centimeters) in diameter. Every so often, the cable and drill bit are removed, and water is poured into the hole. The water and particles at the bottom of the hole are scooped out using a long steel pipe called a bailer.

In rotary drilling, a bit is attached to the end of a series of connected pipes. This is called the drill pipe. As the drill pipe is lowered into the ground, it is rotated, and the bit cuts into the rock. Different bits are used for hard or soft rocks. Mud is pumped down the drill pipe and flows out of the openings in the bit and back up between the pipe and the wall of the hole. This mud cools and cleans the bit, and carries soil and rock from the drill hole to the surface. The pressure of the mud in the well lowers the risk of blowouts and gushers, which are caused by sudden bursts of pressure in an oil reservoir. Blowouts and gushers waste oil and can destroy a rig.

Workers add piping to a Wyoming oil well.

Changing the bit

The drilling crew changes the bit when it becomes dull or if a different type of drill is needed. To change the bit, workers must pull out the entire drill pipe, which may be more than 24,000 feet (7,620 meters) long.

Offshore Operations

Offshore oil explorations are much more difficult and dangerous than oil explorations on land. Crew and equipment must be carried to the site by helicopter or ship. In freezing waters such as the North Sea and the Arctic Ocean, oil rigs may be damaged by storms or ice. It costs about ten times more to set up an offshore rig than it does to build one on land. About one-third of the world's oil comes from offshore oil fields.

Drilling offshore

Drilling an offshore well is like drilling a well on land. The parts of the drilling rig are the same, but the rig must be able to be taken to sea. Wells drilled to explore a site are placed on movable rigs, such as jack-up rigs and semi-submersible rigs, or on drill ships. When oil has been found and a well comes into production, a fixed platform is used.

Jack-up rigs: Jack-up rigs are commonly used in depths of up to 46 feet (60 meters), but they can be used in up to 360 feet (110 meters) of water. Jack-up rigs get their name because they sit on a floating platform attached to steel legs that can be jacked up or down. When the rig is moved, the legs are jacked up off the seafloor, the platform is lowered into the water, and boats tow it to a new site. Once the rig is in position, the legs are lowered again, and the platform is raised above the surface.

Semi-submersible rigs: These are used to explore for oil in depths of up to 3,900 feet (1,200 meters). The rig is mounted on a pontoon suspended just beneath surface of the ocean. Anchors hold the rig in position.

Drill ships use satellite navigation to stay in position over a deep-water well site.

Drill ships: Drill ships are used in water up to 7,800 feet (2,400 meters) deep. The **derrick** and other drilling equipment are mounted on the deck of the drill ship, and the drill pipe is lowered through an opening in the bottom of the ship. Onboard computers take readings from navigation satellites and make careful adjustments using the ship's engines to maintain an exact position over the drilling site.

Production platforms

Production platforms are built and put in position only after explorations have uncovered a reserve of oil large enough to balance the cost. Most fixed platforms are used in shallow water, but they can be used in depths of 980 feet (300 meters) or more.

Production platforms are built in segments that are taken to the drilling site in barges. The bottom segment is guided and lowered to the seafloor with cranes and secured to the seafloor with giant stakes, called piles. A second segment is fitted on top of the bottom segment. Some production platforms have three segments. The top segment is the base for the drilling operations. More than 40 wells can be drilled in different directions from a production platform.

An oil production platform in the North Sea burns off excess gas from the well.

Striking Oil

Drilling for oil is expensive and time-consuming. Throughout the drilling operations, the crew of an oil rig looks carefully for evidence of **petroleum** in the pieces of rock brought up by the drilling mud. When the crew, called riggers, reach a depth where they are likely to find an oil deposit, they carry out further tests.

Testing for oil

Coring involves replacing the drill bit with a coring bit. A coring bit cuts out a cylinder of rock that can be brought up to the surface to be studied. Another test involves lowering measuring instruments, called sondes, into the well hole. Sondes provide information about the composition, fluid content, and other features of the underground rock. Riggers also take samples of fluids and measure their pressure in the drill hole. If they find no evidence of oil, they usually plug the well and abandon it.

Casing

If the crew finds a productive well, they remove the drill pipe and lower a steel casing, or pipe, into the well hole. Then they pump wet cement into the casing and cover it with a special plug that can be drilled through. While the cement is still wet, they pump mud into the casing to push the plug to the bottom. The cement is forced up from the bottom of the hole to the surface, filling the space between the well hole and the outside of the casing. Once the cement has hardened, the riggers can continue drilling through the plug.

Riggers in China work to control a gushing oil well.

The steel casing acts as a protective lining for the well hole, helping to prevent leaks and the possible collapse of the hole. At the top of the casing, the drilling crew installs a a giant valve that closes off the casing if pressure builds in the well.

Moving on to production

Bringing the well into production is carried out in several steps. First, the crew lowers an instrument called a perforator into the casing. When the perforator reaches the depth where the oil has been found, it fires explosive charges into the casing, punching holes into it so the oil can enter it. Next, the crew installs tubing, a string of smaller pipes that brings the oil to the surface. The casing itself would be too wide to get the oil flowing up fast enough.

Finally, the crew puts together a group of control valves at the upper end of the casing and tubing to control the flow of oil to the surface. The crew might find more than one oil-bearing zone where a well has been drilled. If this happens, the crew installs separate tubing and control valves for each zone.

Valves control the flow of lubricants to a North Sea oil rig.

Power Stations

It is hard for us to imagine life without electricity. Electricity heats and lights our homes and provides power for our computers, televisions, refrigerators, and other appliances. Machinery in factories, offices, and hospitals also relies on electric power. All the electricity we use is produced by huge electricity generators in power stations. Most of these power stations burn **fossil fuels** such as coal, oil, or **natural gas** to operate the generators. Fossil-fuel power stations generate more than 60 percent of the world's electric power.

Superheated steam power

In the power stations, the fuel is burned in a combustion chamber to produce heat. This heat is used to change water in a boiler to steam. The steam flows through a set of tubes in a device called a superheater. The temperature and pressure of the steam in the tubes is raised by surrounding the superheater with hot gases from the combustion chamber.

This is the electricity generator inside a coal-burning power station in Montana.

The superheated, high-pressure steam is used to drive a huge steam **turbine.** A steam turbine is made up of a series of wheels, each with many fanlike blades, mounted on a central shaft. As the steam flows through the turbine, it pushes against the blades, causing both the wheels and the turbine shaft to spin. The spinning shaft powers the electricity generator.

An electricity generator has two main parts—a non-moving part called a stator and a turning part called a rotor. In the massive generators used in power stations, the stator is made up of hundreds of coils of copper wire. The rotor is a large **electromagnet.** As the spinning shaft of the turbine turns the rotor, the **magnetic field** created by the rotor turns as the rotor turns. This spinning magnetic field produces a **voltage** in the wire coils of the stator, causing an electric current to flow.

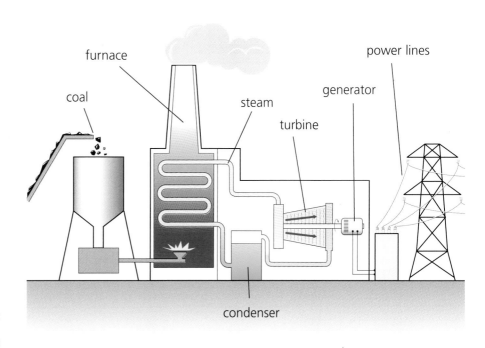

After the steam leaves the turbine, it passes into a condenser. There, it flows around pipes carrying cool water. The heat from the steam is transferred to the water in the pipes. Then the steam cools, condenses into water again, and is pumped back to the boiler in the furnace.

Coal is burned to heat water, which produces steam, which spins a turbine, which turns a generator, which produces electricity that we can use!

Spray ponds and cooling towers

The water in the condenser pipes, which has absorbed heat from the steam, has to be cooled before it can be used again. To do this, the heated water is pumped to a spray pond or a cooling tower. At a spray pond, the water is sprayed out through nozzles. This increases the rate at which it loses heat. In a cooling tower, the water spills down through a series of decks, cooling as it comes into contact with the air. The cooled water may be recycled through the condenser or simply sent into a nearby lake or river or into the sea.

Pollution problems

Fossil-fuel power stations are a reliable way of producing huge amounts of electrical energy. However, they do cause problems. Some power plants give off heated water into the environment, which may harm plant and animal life. Also, the smoke from burning fossil fuels causes air pollution.

Engines: Moving the World

We depend on the internal combustion engine to power all the cars and trucks in the world. A combustion engine burns a mixture of fuel and air and turns **chemical energy** into **heat energy**. The heat energy is then changed into **mechanical energy** to perform useful work.

Gasoline engines

The most common kind of internal combustion engine is the gasoline-powered **piston** engine, which uses gasoline taken from **petroleum.** The rate at which a gasoline engine produces work is usually measured in terms of horsepower or watts.

There are two main types of gasoline engine: reciprocating engines and **rotary** engines. Reciprocating engines have pistons that move up and down or back and forth. A crankshaft turns this reciprocating motion into rotary, or revolving, motion. A rotary engine uses rotors instead of pistons. The rotors produce what is called rotary motion.

Gasoline engines are well-suited to powering vehicles because they are compact and light in weight considering the power they produce. Nearly all cars, motorcycles, and tractors have gasoline engines, as do many trucks, buses, airplanes, and some boats.

An internal combustion engine goes through a four-step process.

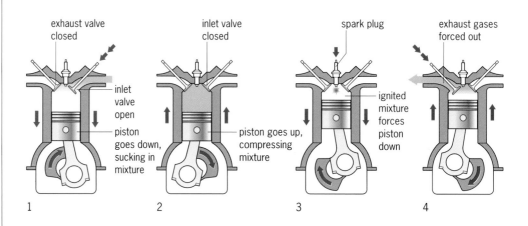

Car engines

Most car engines are made up of several cylinders arranged in one or two rows. Each cylinder contains a piston and a spark plug. A mixture of air and gasoline is forced into the cylinder and is compressed. Then a spark from the spark plug ignites the gasoline mix, pushing the piston along the cylinder. The pistons are connected to a rod, which is called a crankshaft. As a piston slides down the cylinder, it makes the crankshaft turn. The engine is designed so that the pistons are fired down the cylinders one after another. In this way, the crankshaft is kept turning. The crankshaft is connected to the wheels of the car by a series of gears so that the wheels turn as the crankshaft turns. The amount of power the engine produces is managed by a throttle that controls how much air and fuel enter the cylinder.

Diesel engines

Diesel engines are used mainly for heavy-duty work, such as powering trains, freight trucks, and buses. Some cars also use diesel engines. Diesel power is used in ships, submarines, and in emergency electricity generators. Diesel engines are larger and heavier than gasoline engines of comparable power. They burn fuel oils, which, like gasoline, come from petroleum. However, the fuel oils require less refining and are cheaper to produce. The diesel engine compresses the air in the cylinders, causing the air temperature to rise. Fuel is then injected into the hot, compressed air and ignites immediately. The resulting explosion pushes against pistons, forcing them along cylinders to turn a crankshaft.

Near-death experience

The diesel engine was invented by Rudolf Diesel, a German engineer, who patented his design in 1892 and built his first engine in 1893. The engine exploded and almost killed him.

Diesel engines are often used to power large trucks.

Fossil-Fueled Flight

Without **fossil fuels,** air travel would be impossible. An aircraft uses two main types of engines: reciprocating engines and jet engines, which both use fossil fuels.

Piston power

Reciprocating engines, which are also called **piston** engines, are the most widely used type of airplane engine. Although they are not as powerful as jet engines, they are still used in most light aircraft because they work better at low speeds. An aircraft's reciprocating engine is similar to the one found in cars and trucks. Both types burn a fine spray of gasoline and air inside cylinders, using the explosion to drive pistons up and down and to rotate a crankshaft. In an aircraft, the rotating crankshaft turns the propeller. In a car, it makes the wheels spin.

Engine power

The most powerful reciprocating engines ever used on aircraft were the 2722-kilowatt engines of the American B-36 bombers, which flew in the late 1940s.

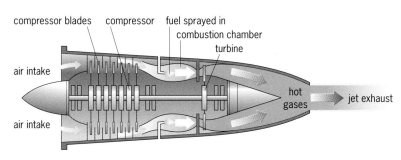

A jet engine has many different parts.

Jet power

The principle of jet propulsion was first described in 1687 by Sir Isaac Newton in his third law of motion, which states that for every action there is an equal and opposite reaction. You can test this by blowing up a balloon and releasing it. Air escaping from the balloon's neck is the action. The equal and opposite reaction is the wayward flight of the balloon around the room. Jet propulsion drives an aircraft engine in much the same way. Gas pressure inside the engine is produced by burning fuel in a combustion chamber. Most jet engines use a liquid **petroleum** fuel similar to kerosene. The gases are directed out through a nozzle as a powerful stream that pushes the engine forward.

Jet engines weigh less than reciprocating engines but produce much greater power. This enables large aircraft to travel long distances at high speeds. There are three main types of jet engines: turbojets; turbofans, or fanjets; and turboprops.

Turbojet: A turbojet takes air in through the front and burns it with fuel to give a powerful jet exhaust that thrusts the aircraft forward. As the jet exhaust passes out through the engine's tail pipe, it spins a **turbine** that turns a compressor, raising the pressure of the air in the engine. The turbojet was the first successful jet engine, and it is still used today.

Turbofans: A turbofan operates somewhat like a turbojet, but it has a fan at the front that draws in air. Part of the air sucked in by the fan is burned with the fuel. The rest is added to the exhaust as it passes from the tail pipe. This results in an exhaust that is much cooler, but more powerful, than that of a turbojet. Turbofans work better at low speeds, are quieter, and use less fuel than turbojets do. Almost all new commercial passenger jets have turbofan engines.

Turboprops: A turboprop is a combination of a turbojet and a propeller. The turboprop is basically a turbojet that uses its power to spin a power turbine that turns a propeller. The energy left in the combustion gases after they have turned the power turbine adds a small amount of jet thrust to the propeller's thrust. A turboprop combines the power of a jet engine and the stability of a propeller aircraft. Turboprops are smaller and lighter than piston engines, but they produce the same amount of power.

The jet engine, which burns fossil fuels, has greatly changed transportation.

Gas guzzlers!

A Boeing 747 can fly for 8,430 miles (9,700 kilometers) on a single load of fuel—57,000 gallons (178,000 liters).

Environmental Impact

Removing **fossil fuels** from the ground and taking them to wherever they are needed damages the environment. In strip mining, earth-moving machines dig holes in the ground, sometimes many miles across, to get at coal **seams.** Waste materials, called spoils, produce acids when they are exposed to rain. Run-off from the strip mines can pollute nearby waterways when rainwater mixed with the acids runs down the bare slopes. This run-off washes away fertile soil.

Strip mining also buries fertile soil under tons of rock. Waste material from deep shaft mines has to be dumped on land or in the ocean. Strip-mined land can be restored by leveling the steep slopes and replacing as much topsoil as possible.

Sometimes mines can settle. Removing large seams of coal from under the ground causes the layers of rock above the coal seam to collapse, causing damage to buildings, roads, and underground pipes and cables. When mines disrupt drainage systems, agriculture can also be affected.

The biggest mines in the world are opencast strip mines where **minerals** are near the surface.

In their search for **petroleum,** oil companies must build roads and temporary structures. In the United States, a great deal of protest has risen about oil exploration in the delicate **ecosystem** of the Arctic tundra. Leaks from wells drilled in shallow coastal waters create oil slicks that pollute beaches and kill sea-life.

Oil spills

In December 1999, the 25-year-old tanker *Erika* broke in two, spilling more than 10,000 tons of fuel oil on French beaches. This is just one of a number of incidents in which coastlines have been badly polluted by oil spills.

The U.S. government enacted the Oil Pollution Act (OPA) in 1990 after the *Exxon Valdez* ran aground, causing a huge oil spill. The accident caused a great deal of environmental damage in Alaska. The OPA demands the use of double-hulled vessels, which are believed to lower the chances of pollution in low-impact collisions or groundings. Operators have been given until 2015 to upgrade their fleets.

After January 1, 2010, single-hull oil tankers weighing above a certain amount will not be able to enter European ports if proposed regulations become law. Although all new tankers have been built with double hulls since 1996, the new regulations would affect up to 50 percent of ships.

Volunteers begin the difficult task of cleaning up after an oil spill on the coast of France.

Oil spills waiting to happen?

In 1997, eleven billion barrels of refined oil products were transported globally by sea.

Air Pollution and Climate Change

The major sources of air pollution are cars, trucks, buses, factories, and **fossil-fuel** power stations. Air pollution poisons the air with chemicals that can cause damage to **ecosystems** and are dangerous to people's health.

Acid rain

Acid rain is caused when chemicals from vehicle exhausts and coal-burning power stations dissolve in water in the atmosphere to form sulfuric and nitric acids. This makes rain, snow, and fog more acidic than usual. Air currents can carry the acid many miles away from the site of the pollution, where it falls and damages crops, trees, lakes, and buildings.

Many lakes in Scandinavia, the northeastern United States, and Canada are so acidic that fish can no longer live there. Acid rain can turn buildings and statues black and can damage them by corroding metal, stone, and paint. Monuments and statues that have survived erosion by the weather for hundreds of years are suddenly being eaten away.

The greenhouse effect

Earth's atmosphere contains gases called **greenhouse gases.** In a greenhouse, the Sun's rays pass through the glass, but its **heat energy** cannot pass back out. Greenhouse gases work in a similar way. They let the Sun's rays pass through to the surface of the planet, but they prevent the heat reflected back from Earth's surface from being radiated into space. As a result, the atmosphere gradually warms up.

These trees in Poland have been damaged by acid rain.

Carbon dioxide, a greenhouse gas, is present naturally in the atmosphere. However, burning fossil fuels also produces carbon dioxide. It causes the carbon dioxide trapped beneath the ground in coal and oil reserves to be given off into the atmosphere at an enormous rate. Burning fossil fuels and deforestation give off about seven billion tons of carbon dioxide each year. Natural processes, such as the use of carbon dioxide by trees, remove about half of this, but the remaining 3.5 billion tons stay in the atmosphere for 50 to 200 years. Because of this, the amount of carbon dioxide in the atmosphere keeps increasing.

Many scientists believe that rising levels of carbon dioxide and other greenhouse gases are causing Earth's climate to become warmer. This effect is called global warming. Global warming could make the climate so warm that some of the polar ice caps would melt, causing the sea levels to rise. Also, the water in the oceans will expand as it is heated. The worst effects of global warming could bring terrible floods and storms to many parts of the world as weather patterns change.

Many countries are working to decrease air pollution. For example, people are developing vehicles that use less fuel. More power stations and factories are installing filters on their smokestacks to trap harmful chemicals before they can enter the atmosphere.

Heavy traffic clogs the roads of Mexico City. Cars are one of the worst causes of air pollution throughout the world.

Nonrenewable Resources

Fossil fuels are **nonrenewable resources.** This means that once they have been used up, they cannot be replaced. As we have seen, the formation of fossil fuels is a continuing process, but it takes many millions of years to get from plant and animal life to coal, **petroleum,** and **natural gas.** We are using these resources much faster than natural processes are replacing them. The world depends very heavily on fossil fuels, and a great deal of effort will have to be made to find alternatives. Ordinary people can play a part, too, by saving energy. If we use less electricity, less coal will have to be burned to produce it. If we walk or ride bikes instead of driving cars everywhere, we will use less gasoline, cut down on pollution, and save natural resources.

A technician studies data that may help him find the exact location of an oil field.

Crisis? What crisis?

During the oil crisis of the 1970s, people panicked when they began to believe that the oil supplies were running dry and prices would go up forever. Between 1973 and 1998, world oil consumption rose by around 25 percent to 26 billion barrels a year. At the same time, production at oil reserves using existing technology jumped more than 50 percent to 1 trillion barrels.

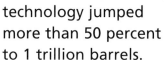

One reason for this increase in production is that there was a huge improvement in the technology used to find oil reserves. For example, computers can be used to make seismic maps of underground formations, thereby improving the chances of finding oil. The development of horizontal drilling techniques means that more oil can be recovered from known fields.

A traditional, vertically-drilled hole taps an oil reservoir at only one spot. However, a horizontal drill can run along the length of a reservoir, allowing the oil to be removed more easily. New deep-water drilling techniques have opened new fields, because oil companies can now drill in waters five times deeper than they could a few years ago.

Energy alternatives

Scientists and engineers are exploring renewable energy sources that might take the place of fossil fuel. These include solar energy, wind power, wave power, hydroelectric power, and **geothermal energy.**

Coal

Coal supplies are not under quite as much pressure as oil supplies are. Coal is still an important resource, because it provides about 25 percent of the world's energy needs. However, we still have an ample supply of coal. At current rates of production and consumption, the world's coal reserves should last for more than 230 years. Oil reserves, on the other hand, are expected to begin to run out in 40 years. Also, coal reserves are evenly spread across Asia, Europe, and the U.S. This differs from oil, which is in the hands of just a few major producers.

China, for example, has very large coal reserves. However, most of these are in the north, and the greatest energy demand is in the south. Because it is difficult to transport coal by land in China, they import about 50 million tons of coal a year. Australia is one of the largest exporters of high-quality coal in the world. Recently, big companies from the United States, Great Britain, and South Africa have been buying shares in Australian coal-mining businesses.

A train carries a fresh supply of coal to a power station.

Fuel Wars

Today, oil provides almost half of the world's energy needs. If every nation that used oil could produce enough to meet its own needs, things would be fairly simple. However, this is not the case. Nations that use large amounts of oil do not necessarily produce large amounts. Countries such as France and Japan, which use large amounts of oil but have no supplies of their own, have always imported their oil.

During the 1970s, the United States went from being able to provide its own oil to having to import more than half of its oil supplies. All of these oil troubles came about with the creation of the Organization of **Petroleum** Exporting Countries (OPEC), a group of the major oil-producing nations, which did not include Mexico, the United States, or the former Soviet Union.

OPEC takes control

In the 1960s, the OPEC countries began to take over the control of their own oil production from private oil companies. By the early 1970s, OPEC had raised prices of **crude oil** so high that they affected the economies of all oil-importing countries, especially developing ones. Oil-dependent countries, such as Japan, faced economic slumps. Higher prices for petroleum-based fertilizers meant that the cost of food production rose, too. Because developed countries were paying higher prices for oil imports, they had less money to spend on importing goods from developing countries. At the same time, developing countries had to pay more for imported goods because the cost of manufacturing rose with the increase in energy prices.

At the first sign of an energy crisis, motorists tend to buy in a panic, further draining fuel reserves.

The effects that energy has on the world economy show how dependent we are on maintaining our supplies of it. Because coal reserves are much larger and more widely available than petroleum, it is unlikely that an organization could control coal production in the way that OPEC controls the oil supply. However, increased use of coal will cause severe pollution problems.

A volatile situation

In 1998, oil prices dropped by about 50 percent. An economic crisis in Asia slowed demand, while a mild winter in the United States had the same effect. Misreading the signs, OPEC increased production and found that it had far more oil than people wanted. The United States postponed or canceled exploration and drilling projects and 65,000 people lost their jobs. Other oil-producing nations also suffered huge losses.

In March 1999, OPEC cut oil production by 1.7 million barrels a day. Four nations not in OPEC—Mexico, Russia, Norway, and Oman—also agreed to cut their combined output by 400,000 barrels a day. Finally, demand for oil increased as Asia recovered from its economic crisis.

The problem is that two-thirds of the world's known oil reserves lie in the Middle East—a region known for its turmoil. Who knows what future events might disrupt the flow of fuel to the world?

Fuel alternatives

Japan is less dependent on oil than it was in the 1970s. More than a third of Japan's electricity is now supplied by nuclear reactors, compared with just 6.5 percent during the 1970s oil crisis. Industries such as computer software development are growing in Japan, while oil-demanding industries, such as steel manufacturing, are less important.

At the end of the Gulf War in 1991, the oil fields of Kuwait were devastated by retreating Iraqi troops.

Fossil Fuel Statistics

World oil production

Countries with the largest proven crude oil reserves, 1996

(in millions of barrels)

Saudi Arabia	261,444
Iraq	112,000
United Arab Emirates	97,800
Kuwait	96,500
Iran	92,600

Countries with the greatest oil production, 1996

(in millions of barrels per day)

Saudi Arabia	8.1
Former Soviet Union	6.9
United States	6.5
Iran	3.6
China	3.2

- At the end of 1996, OPEC had proven reserves of 801,998 million barrels of **crude oil.** This amounts to 76.6 percent of the world total.

- There are 11 members of the OPEC group. They are Algeria, Indonesia, Iran, Iraq, Kuwait, Libya, Nigeria, Qatar, Saudi Arabia, United Arab Emirates, and Venezuela.

- The total world usage of crude oil in 1996 was 71.7 million barrels per day. There are 42 gallons (159 liters) in a barrel.

Natural gas production	billion yard^3/year*	billion meter^3/year**
Russia	837	640
United States	661	505
Canada	167	128
Netherlands	114	87

*yard^3/year means "cubic yards per year"
**meter^3/year means "cubic meters per year"

World energy production

Energy is measured in joules. In the following tables, figures are given in terajoules (tJ). One terajoule is a billion joules. A bolt of lightning unleashes around 0.003 terajoules of energy.

Energy production, 1998	
United States	76.6 million tJ
Russia	41.9 million tJ
China	39.5 million tJ
Saudi Arabia	21.5 million tJ
Canada	18.2 million tJ
Great Britain	12.1 million tJ

Energy consumption, 1998	
United States	98.5 million tJ
China	39.0 million tJ
Russia	27.4 million tJ
Japan	22.6 million tJ
Germany	15.2 million tJ
Canada	12.9 million tJ
India	12.2 million tJ
Great Britain	10.6 million tJ

Glossary

acid rain rain that contains sulfur dioxide from coal burning and nitrogen oxides from car exhausts and other sources

atom smallest unit of matter that can take part in a chemical reaction; smallest part of an element that can exist

carbohydrate major class of food, including some sugars, starches, and plant fibers

cell smallest unit of life

chemical energy energy in the bonds that hold atoms together in molecules that is given off during a chemical reaction

coke solid fuel that is about 90 percent carbon and is made by heating coal in an airtight oven to remove impurities; most commonly used fuel in the iron and steel industries

compound chemical substance made up of two or more atoms of different elements bonded together

crude oil raw form of petroleum

decomposer animal that breaks down the remains of other animals and plants

derrick tower used for hoisting drill pipes

ecosystem community of living organisms and their nonliving environment

electromagnet magnet produced by passing an electric current through a wire wrapped around an iron core

fossil fuel fuel produced through the action of heat and pressure on the fossil remains of plants and animals that lived millions of years ago

geologist scientist who studies the origin, history, and structure of Earth

geophysicist scientist who studies the branch of physics concerned with Earth and its environment

geothermal energy energy taken from the hot rocks and water beneath Earth's surface

gravity force of attraction at the surface of a planet

greenhouse gas gas in the atmosphere, such as carbon dioxide or methane, that prevents heat radiated from Earth's surface from escaping into space

heat energy energy created by moving atoms and molecules

heating value measure of the amount of energy produced when a fuel is burned

hydraulic jack device powered by water pressure and used for lifting heavy weights

impervious can't be penetrated

Industrial Revolution period of history from around 1740 to 1850 when economic and social life was changed by the introduction of coal-powered steam engines to power machines for manufacturing

ion charged particle that forms during a chemical change

magnetic field region around a magnet in which a force acts on another magnet or on a moving electric charge

mechanical energy amount of work that an object can do

microorganism living thing that is too small to be seen without a microscope

mineral naturally occurring substance with a definite chemical composition and a characteristic structure; any valuable substance removed from the ground

molecule two or more atoms joined by chemical bonds; if the atoms are the same, it is an element; if they are different, it is a compound

natural gas substance often found along with petroleum deposits within layers of sedimentary rock that can be used as fuel; including methane, propane, and butane

nonporous having few tiny holes or pores through which fluids can pass

nonrenewable resource resource that cannot be replaced after it is used up or can be replaced only over thousands or millions of years

offshore located in the ocean or sea, away from the coastline

organic coming from living or once-living organisms

peat compacted plant remains that have partly decayed in conditions of low oxygen

petroleum thick, liquid mixture found underground, formed by the action of bacteria and the forces of high pressure and temperature on the remains of marine plants and animals over millions of years

photosynthesis process by which green plants and some other organisms use the energy of the Sun to make sugars from carbon dioxide and water

piston sliding piece inside an engine that is moved by fluid pressure

rotary relating to rotation or spinning

salt dome underground structure composed of a core of salt, often about 1/2 mile (3/4 kilometer) or more in diameter, and the surrounding layers of rock that form a cap, or dome, over it

sedimentary rock rock formed over millions of years by the accumulation of layer upon layer of sediments deposited by wind, water, or ice

seam underground layer of a mineral such as coal

smelt to remove a metal by heating the rock in which the metal is found to a high temperature

seepage place where petroleum seeps out of the ground

turbine engine in which a fluid is used to spin a shaft by pushing on angled blades; used to spin electricity generators

voltage measurement of the force that moves an electric current around a circuit

More Books to Read

Gibson, Diane. *Fossil Fuels.* North Mankato, Minn.: Smart Apple Media, 2001.

Graham, Ian. *Fossil Fuels.* Austin, Tex.: Raintree Steck-Vaughn, 1999.

Oxlade, Chris. *Energy.* Chicago: Heinemann Library, 1999.

Snedden, Robert. *Energy.* Chicago: Heinemann Library, 1999.

Index